MYSTERIOUS MONSTERS

John Townsend

www.raintreepublishers.co.uk
Visit our website to find out more information about **Raintree** books.

To order:
 Phone 44 (0) 1865 888113
 Send a fax to 44 (0) 1865 314091
 Visit the Raintree Bookshop at **www.raintreepublishers.co.uk** to browse our catalogue and order online.

First published in Great Britain by Raintree Publishers, Halley Court, Jordan Hill, Oxford OX2 8EJ, part of Harcourt Education Ltd. Raintree is a registered trademark of Harcourt Education Ltd.

Editorial: Charlotte Guillain and Isabel Thomas
Design: Michelle Lisseter and Bridge Creative Services Ltd
Picture Research: Maria Joannou and Kay Altwegg
Production: Jonathan Smith
Index: Indexing Specialists (UK) Ltd

Originated by Ambassador
Printed and bound in China

ISBN 1 844 43215 7 (hardback)
08 07 06 05 04
10 9 8 7 6 5 4 3 2 1

ISBN 1 844 43225 4 (paperback)
09 08 07 06 05
10 9 8 7 6 5 4 3 2 1

A full catalogue record for this book is available from the British Library.

Acknowledgements

Page 04–05, Ronald Grant Archive/; 04, Ronald Grant Archive/; 06–07, Ronald Grant Archive/; 07, Ronald Grant Archive/; 06, Oxford Scientific Films/; 06, NHPA/; 08–09, Ronald Grant Archive/; 08, NHPA/; 09, Oxford Scientific Films/; 10–11, Ronald Grant Archive/; 10, Science Photo Library/; 11, Kobal Collection/20th Century Fox Television; 12–13, Ronald Grant Archive/; 12, Mary Evans Picture Library/; 13, Corbis/; 14–15, NHPA/; 15, Digital Stock/; 16, NHPA; 17, Gondwana Studios, The Queen Victoria Museum, Tasmania; 18–19, John Cleare Mountain Photography/; 19, Topham Picturepoint/; 20 right, Fortean Picture Library/; 20–21, Fortean Picture Library/Patterson/ Gimlin; 22 right, Fortean Picture Library/; 22 left, Fortean Picture Library/; 23, Corbis/ Jacques Langevin; 25 left, NHPA/; 24, Fortean Picture Library/; 25 right, Corbis/; 27, Topham Picturepoint/; 26, Corbis/; 28–29, Oxford Scientific Films/; 28, Topham Picturepoint/; 29, Topham Picturepoint/; 30–31, Corbis/; 30, Fortean Picture Library/; 31, Fortean Picture Library/; 32–33, Natural History Museum/; 32, Corbis/; 33, Corbis/; 34–35, Fortean Picture Library/; 34, Corbis/; 35, Corbis/; 36–37, Topham Pitcurepoint/ Charlie Walker Collection; 36, NHPA/; 37, Corbis/; 38–39, Nature Force/ Australian Museum; 38, Topham Picturepoint/; 39, /Wm Leo Smith; 40–41, NHPA/ Haroldo Palo Jr; 42–43, NHPA/; 42, Corbis/New Zealand Herald; 43, Fortean Picture Library; 44, Corbis/Karl Ammann; 44–45, Fortean Picture Library ; 46, NHPA/; 47, Natural History Museum ; 48–49, NHPA/; 48, Corbis/Galen Rowell; 50 left, Kobal Collection/; 50 right, Mary Evans Picture Library/; 51, Ronald Grant Archive/; 51, Corbis/; 14, Corbis/Bob Krist. Cover photograph reproduced with permission of Getty Images/Imagebank.

Every effort has been made to contact copyright holders of any material reproduced in this book. Any omissions will be rectified in subsequent printings if notice is given to the publishers.

Disclaimer

CONTENTS

Any words appearing in the text in bold, **like this**, are explained in the Glossary. You can also look out for them in the Weird words box at the bottom of each page.

MONSTERS RULE!

MONSTERS GO BACK A LONG WAY

We have always found monsters creepy. This is probably because:

- Thousands of years ago people told stories of creatures that ate us alive.
- Children's fairy stories are full of evil giants or hungry wolves.
- The latest computer games feature battles against scary beasts.

Some of the first stories people ever told were of scary beasts. Since humans first sat around fires to tell stories, monsters have been the stuff of **folklore**.

People would tell stories of dragons breathing fire. They talked about giant man-eating birds. They drew huge **serpents** in the mud. Great **myths** grew from these weird and wonderful stories about monsters.

All around the world, people still talk about strange beasts in secret places. After all, there are many **remote** places just right for a monster to hide in.

King Kong is one of the most famous movie monsters.

WEIRD WORDS   folklore   old beliefs, myths and stories
myth   made-up tale, told over many years

SCARY STORIES

A giant **reptile** creeps up from the sewers. A fierce wolfman claws at the door. A huge **dinosaur** attacks the city. We still love monster movies and videos that make us scream.

The **ancient** Greeks were just the same. They loved monster stories full of fear and danger. If the hero killed the terrible beast, people were happy because it was like good overcoming evil.

Mystery beasts make great stories. But do monsters really exist? Or are they just made up for a bit of excitement? Maybe some monsters are really **lurking** in secret places. Read on and make up your own mind… if you dare!

FIND OUT LATER...

Are living dinosaurs still out there?

Do water dragons really hide in lakes and seas?

What if monsters still hide in the mountains?

remote   far away from people
serpent   large snake

MONSTERS OF MYTH AND FICTION

The hippogryph makes a good taxi for Harry Potter in *The Prisoner of Azkaban.*

Monsters in the movies make money. They are good for **business** and sell millions of videos. People in the 21st century still love weird creatures and new ones are being created all the time. Today with the help of special effects, teeth seem to bite us from the screen.

It could be a troll or an orc in *The Lord of the Rings*. From *Eight-Legged Freaks* to *Shrek* or *The Incredible Hulk* – we are mad about strange beasts. Maybe there is a need in all of us to believe in monsters. They help us face the real troubles in life. After we tremble at the Basilisk on the screen, our real-life problems do not seem so bad after all.

HIPPOGRYPH

Some beasts of **myth** are a bit of a mix! The hippogryph has the hind legs of a horse, with the body and wings of a gryphon. A gryphon is part lion, part eagle. It comes from old European myths.

The *Creature From The Black Lagoon* is a horror movie made in 1954. This is the Gill-Man.

WEIRD WORDS   business   trade for making money
glinted   sparkle with light

HOME-MADE MONSTER

*The body lay on the table under a sheet. Lightning flashed in the night sky. Wires crackled and fizzed. Thunder cracked… as the brain sparked into life. Slowly the eyes opened. The sheet slid to the floor as the creature **stirred**. It sat upright on the table. A flash lit the room in a streak of silver. It **glinted** from the bolt in the monster's neck…*

Frankenstein is the famous story of a human monster that still scares people today. Frankenstein made his creature from dead human body parts, in the hope of creating life. When his monster attacked with super-human strength, it was time to run…

FRANKENSTEIN'S MONSTER

Mary Shelley wrote the novel *Frankenstein* in 1816. Nothing like this had been written before. It was not until 1931 that Hollywood made the first film. The actor Boris Karloff played the monster.

Many people think *Frankenstein* is the best horror film ever made. ❯❯

WEREWOLVES

In the days when wolves hunted in most woods and hills, humans had to beware. People's fear of wolves was very real. But there were stories of something even worse. A beast that was half-man, half-wolf.

Such beliefs came from the **Dark Ages**. As soon as a full Moon appeared, the wolfman would turn into a real wolf and hunt for human blood. If one of these wolves bit you, you would become a werewolf too. On the night of a full Moon you would start to change. Your teeth would get sharper. You would grow hair on your hands and face. When you saw the Moon you would throw back your head and howl!

A wolf's howl at night can send a shiver down your spine.

THE WOLF

A wolf is hardly a monster. Not on its own. Yet when our imaginations take over, this night hunter can chill our blood. This is the power of **fiction**.

Dark Ages   over 1000 years ago, when people knew little about the world or science

ONCE BITTEN

The **legend** of humans turning into wolves goes back hundreds of years to the forests of Europe. It may have begun with the disease **rabies**. Anyone bitten by a wild dog with rabies would soon froth at the mouth and growl with fever. It seemed like they were turning into a wild animal. There was no cure.

Stories spread about people being bitten and turning into beasts. If they became a werewolf, there was nothing they could do. Each full Moon they needed to kill. They would turn into a savage monster and run into the night with a thirst for human blood…

HOW TO BECOME A WEREWOLF

Many ancient beliefs came from Italy. You could be a werewolf if:

- *you were born on a Friday under a full Moon*
- *you slept with the full Moon shining on your face*
- *you drank water from the footprint of a savage wolf.*

Strange things happen during a full Moon. ❝❝

legend story from long ago that may be partly true
rabies disease caught from the bite of an infected animal

DEALING WITH VAMPIRES

According to some beliefs, if you sleep with garlic and a silver knife under your bed, you will keep both vampires and werewolves away. But if you want to slay one, nothing less than a wooden **stake** right through the heart will do.

Can we trust people who do not like garlic? They may be vampires!

VAMPIRES

The **legend** said that when a werewolf died, it would return as a vampire. The two monsters went side by side in many early stories. Today, vampires and the people who **slay** them appear all the time on television. For years, horror films have scared millions of people with the dripping fangs and red eyes of the 'undead'.

The fear of vampires was very real a few hundred years ago. Legends of blood-sucking creatures came from all round the world. In China, vampires had green or pink hair. Greek vampires had a woman's body and the tail of a winged **serpent**. The stories said that if they bit you, you would turn into a vampire forever.

Dracula is the most famous vampire. >>

prey   hunt down to kill
slay   kill

DRACULA

In 1897 Bram Stoker wrote a book based on the vampire stories. Count Dracula became a modern **myth** and many films have been made about him. Most people today think of a vampire as a blood-drinking man who can change into a bat. He wears a black cape, has black slicked-back hair, a deathly pale face and fangs. He **preys** on his human victims at night by sucking blood from the veins in the side of their necks. He cannot stand sunlight and sleeps in a coffin in a basement. He has no shadow. But would you call him a monster? You might if he stood by your bed tonight!

Buffy has made vampire stories popular again.

BUFFY THE VAMPIRE SLAYER

Who would have thought vampire slaying could be a big TV hit?

66 Buffy, when I said you could slay vampires and have a life, I didn't mean at the same time! 99

Giles

66 I don't like vampires. I'm going to take a stand and say they're not good. 99

Xander

THE WORLD OF DRAGONS

Ancient stories say that if you meet a dragon, you are as good as dead. It could spit out fire and eat you ready cooked.

Our deep fear of being eaten alive could explain many of our monster **myths**. But dragons might be more than a myth. Perhaps there was a creature living long ago that started the stories about dragons. Otherwise, why would people from different parts of the world tell of similar beasts with **scales**, long tails and claws? Whether they were the dragons of Greek myths or the Bible, they could be very scary. Strangely, the dragons of ancient China were believed to be friendly.

GEORGE AND THE DRAGON

One hero who saved a beautiful girl from a dragon's jaws was Saint George. He killed the evil dragon – a **triumph** over the powers of darkness.

Legends say that the only way to keep a dragon away is to feed it a **maiden**.

WEIRD WORDS   fossils   ancient remains of animal bones and teeth
maiden   young unmarried woman

LONG AGO

So what is a dragon like? Most stories say that a dragon:

- is like a **reptile**
- breathes fire or poison
- lives in or near water
- can fly.

In many stories, it was the dragon's job to guard treasure or a special place or person. Most dragons were big and powerful. It was not wise to argue with a dragon.

So where did all these ideas come from? Could a beast like this really have lived? Did any **survive** from the age of the **dinosaurs**? Perhaps ancient people did see flying monsters. It was only in the 19th century that **fossils** proved that huge flying lizards did once exist. Maybe some still do. But nowadays people are more likely to claim to have seen aliens than dragons.

In the latest Godzilla film, computer animation was used to create a truly terrifying monster.

Did fire-breathing dragons once roam the Earth?

GODZILLA

Godzilla has been a film star for over fifty years. It keeps coming back to scare the world. The dragon-like monster was just a rubber model in the early films. But it still made some people in cinemas faint.

scales small bony plates that protect the skin
triumph success and victory

Sometimes it pays not to get too close to wildlife! ⌃⌃

MAN-EATER

In 1973 Baron Rudolph sat down to relax while his tour group went to explore the island. He was not seen again. A Komodo dragon ate him. All that was left was his blood-stained shirt and camera. Other tourists have since gone the same way.

KOMODO DRAGON

You hear a sound in the grass. There is a bad smell in the air. Branches spring apart and suddenly something runs towards you. It is huge, with cold eyes and open jaws. Sharp long teeth drip with deadly **saliva.** The monster flicks out a red tongue like a flame.

No one knew about these creatures a hundred years ago. Dragons were only supposed to be **myths.** Or they were **extinct** beasts from another age. But in 1912 a pilot crash-landed on the island of Komodo in Indonesia. He was shocked when he saw the biggest lizard in the world. At 3 metres long, it was one of the surprises of the 20th century.

Komodo dragons are very rare. There are only a few thousand left in the world. Because of this they are now a protected **species.** ⌃⌃

ambush   surprise attack
boar   large wild pig

KILLERS

Komodo dragons can eat almost their own weight in meat in one sitting. They wait to **ambush** their victims. Despite this, they can run as fast as a human. They rush out from their hiding place and tear a bite from their victim. That is enough. The dragon's mouth is deadly because its teeth are full of rotting meat. This is what makes it smell so foul. A bite will poison the victim, who will soon die.

The Komodo dragon hunts mostly wild **boar** and deer, but it will have a go at any animal around on the island. This may be another Komodo dragon, or even a person. It does not seem to mind.

SIZE

A large Komodo dragon can be twice the size and weight of a human. Maybe that does not make it a real monster like the dragons of myths. But what if it had bigger members in its family? Could they still be out there somewhere?

Komodo dragons can give victims a deadly bite.

extinct   died out, never to return
saliva   mouth juices, spit

15

CLOSE FAMILY

The largest known Australian lizard is far too small to be mistaken for its big 'dragon' cousins. At 2 metres long, even on a dark night, a monitor lizard would hardly look like Megalania.

This large monitor lizard eats fish and small mammals.

MEGALANIA

The Megalania was a real monster. Some people say it is still alive. It would probably act like a giant Komodo dragon on the **prowl**. At up to 10 metres long it would have been five times heavier than a Komodo dragon. That is really big – and far more dangerous than today's biggest crocodile.

The mystery is whether Megalania died out in the last ice age 20,000 years ago. Many people say they have seen one alive in the **Australian bush**. Some have found footprints in the mud that they believe is **evidence** this monster still exists. But the footprints could well be from a very large Komodo dragon, alive and well in the Australian outback. If it is a Megalania, people had better watch out.

Part of a Megalania skeleton has been made up from **fossils** found at sites across Australia. The beasts would look a bit like this.

Australian bush   Australia's wild country, with desert, scrub land and swamps

SIGHTINGS

Many years ago an Australian farmer saw a huge lizard moving along the edge of his field. He used a set of fence posts and worked out that the animal's length was over 8 metres. That is bigger than a 2-tonne saltwater crocodile.

In 1961 three woodcutters were scared by a huge lizard. They guessed it was about 7 metres long. That is much bigger than the biggest Komodo dragon on record.

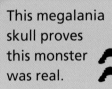

This megalania skull proves this monster was real.

Frank Gordon was a scientist who studied **reptiles**. In 1979 he was out in the mountains of New South Wales in Australia. His car disturbed something that looked like a log. It stirred and then suddenly ran off. It was a lizard about 10 metres long.

Could these lizards have been Megalania?

If the Megalania still exists, why has none been caught? Maybe it is because:

1 they keep out of sight

2 they hunt at night

3 they lie still and look like logs.

After all, Komodo dragons have only recently been discovered.

evidence   information that can help prove if something is true or false

17

MYSTERY BEASTS OF THE MOUNTAINS

WHAT DOES THE YETI LOOK LIKE?

Everyone who has seen the yeti gives the same description:

* it has long dark hair
* it is like an ape with no tail
* it walks upright like a man but is much bigger
* it has a strong, **vile** smell.

There may be a monster hiding in mountains around the world. This monster has many names. But whatever people call the hairy ape-man, climbers keep reporting that it really is out there.

THE YETI

The mountains around Mount Everest are **bleak** and empty. Unless you believe the stories that say something lives there. We call the mountain monster the **abominable** snowman. Local people of Tibet and Nepal call him 'yah-teh' or yeti. Yeti means 'that thing of the mountains'.

Many attempts have been made to find a yeti. But it is like looking for a needle in a haystack. This is a **vast** wild country, where the **habitat** is rocky, icy and very high up. It is very **hostile** to people.

DNA   individual code locked in the genes that shows the make-up of a creature

A LUCKY ESCAPE

In 1974 a girl was alone in the mountains looking after her **yaks**. Suddenly she heard a loud grunt and a yeti came running towards her. She tried to run but the yeti grabbed her. There was nothing she could do but scream. Luckily the yeti dropped her in a stream and grabbed one of the yaks. It seemed to be in a rage. It easily killed the yak with its bare hands and the girl ran home in terror. When the police came they found large footprints in the snow but no yeti was to be seen. The yeti seems to be very good at escaping and hiding.

PROOF?

Is there any proof that the yeti exists? Look at the **evidence**:

- sightings over hundreds of years
- fuzzy photos of an ape-man
- huge footprints in the snow
- yaks have been killed and their bodies left half-eaten
- **DNA** tests on hair match no known animal.

This hand is thought to have come from a yeti skeleton. It is kept in a monastery at the foot of Mount Everest in Nepal.

Were these huge footprints made by a yeti?

habitat   natural home or environment
yak   long-haired mountain ox

BIGFOOT FACTS

What makes us so sure there is really a Bigfoot out there? Perhaps because:

- people have reported seeing hairy man-like beasts in mountains and the wilderness in North America for over 400 years
- reports keep coming in from **reliable** people who are convinced they have seen a Bigfoot
- for over 70 years people have found sets of large human-shaped tracks in **remote** areas.

These plaster casts were taken of huge footprints found in mud. **>>**

MYSTERY APE-MAN

The hills and forests of North America may hide the mountain monster, too.

Native Americans have told stories of 'the big hairy man' for hundreds of years. Some call him Sasquatch and others call him Bigfoot.

Some Native American tribes see him as an elder brother who keeps a friendly eye on them. They say he knows when people go looking for him so he hides in the mountains. Very few people have managed to find him or film him yet. But it may not be long before someone finds real proof, one way or the other. Is Bigfoot real or a big **hoax**?

hoax   untrue story made up for a joke
hostile   unfriendly or against you

MANY SIGHTINGS

Reports say that Bigfoot can have black, red or grey hair. Some people say he is shy and harmless but others say he is **hostile**.

Here a man describes what he saw in Kentucky in the USA in 2003. He was driving on Highway 92 near the town of Pine Knot.

'I saw something ahead at the side of the road. Maybe it was a deer so I slowed down. As I got close, I was shocked. It was over 2 metres tall and covered in grey hair. It looked at me with big red eyes. It seemed to be angry. I was scared to death and drove off fast.'

FAMOUS FILM

Roger Patterson shot a famous film in 1967. He was on a horse when he came across Bigfoot. Or so he said. Some people think it is a hoax but others think it is real. It is the only movie film of Bigfoot in all these years.

Shots from Roger Patterson's film.

reliable sensible and trustworthy

TERROR

Even fierce dogs are said to tremble if a yowie is near. Many campers have seen a hairy visitor at night raiding bins. It eats anything, even kangaroos! Then it staggers off with a terrifying cry and that **vile** smell.

YOWIE AND ALMA

The Australian **Aborigines** have told stories for thousands of years. One of the stories is about a hairy 'evil spirit' called Yowie that lived in the forests and hills. But is this just **folklore** or is Yowie alive and well today? Could Yowie be Australia's own Bigfoot?

Over the last hundred years, many people in Australia say they have seen Yowie. Reports come from Queensland and New South Wales all the time.

Yowie is supposed to be about 2.3 metres tall, with long brown hair. It makes a grunting noise and its **stench** is worse than rotten eggs. Stories say that Yowie's eyes glow yellow in the moonlight.

Yowies are thought to have massive feet and hands. **««**

TALL BEAST OR A TALL STORY?

Yeti, Bigfoot and Yowie all sound like similar monsters. All the other ape-men from around the world sound the same too. They are all a similar size, shape and smell and live in the same kinds of places. Their footprints look the same, too. Could they all be just a **hoax**?

Alma is another member of the family. It lives in the forests and hills of Russia and China. Alma's fur is white up in the mountains but brown in the forests.

In 1997 many Alma footprints were studied in China. Each print was 36 centimetres long. Experts said a creature of over 200 kilograms and at least 2 metres tall must have made them.

A RECENT LEGEND

Hunters caught a wild ape-woman in Russia in the 19th century. They called her Zana and kept her in a cage. She became tame but hated to be indoors. She died in 1890. Some say she was an Alma.

Yowie and Alma can survive the coldest of winters thanks to their thick, wooly coats. A snow drift is no match for them. «

A sign in Washington State, USA, warns of Bigfoot crossing the road. »

stench   foul smell

23

MONSTERS OF THE SKY

GIANT BIRD OF THUNDER

Thunderbirds that carry humans away are part of Native American **folklore**. The birds have been described as having wingspans of over 10 metres, hooked **talons** and razor-sharp beaks.

Are there really monster birds up in the sky that could carry off a human? It sounds like **fantasy**, but maybe it could happen.

MONSTER BIRDS

Large eagles have been known to carry away baby deer that weigh up to 15 kilograms. Some are believed to snatch human babies. In 1868 a teacher in Missouri watched in horror as an eagle grabbed an eight-year-old boy from the school playground. It lifted him high into the air and dropped him to his death.

If an eagle could do this, what about a monster bird twice the size? Such birds once flew in parts of the world. According to some people, they still do.

Could a giant eagle grab a child with its sharp talons? **>>**

The Native Americans of Illinois call the thunderbird a Piasa Monster Bird. The bird has been part of folklore for hundreds of years, as shown on this magazine cover. **<<**

fantasy   from the world of dreams and imagination
talons   claws of a bird of prey

ON THE WINGS OF STORMS

Any bird with a 6-metre wingspan would need strong **thermal air currents** to keep it in the sky. A moving storm sucks up air into the clouds, creating these currents. A huge bird is said to arrive when these storms break out. Its name is Thunderbird. Many reports say such a bird has been spotted in Illinois in the USA.

In 1977, two giant birds appeared in the sky above Lawndale, Illinois. One of them grabbed ten-year-old Marlon Lowe. His mother screamed as the bird lifted him into the air. He hit the bird and it dropped him nearby before flying off. He was left shocked and scratched. Experts say no known American bird would do this.

WINGED MONSTER IN THE HUACHUCA DESERT

In 1890 a cowboy called Jimmy Bradshaw said he was attacked by a thunderbird as he rode in the desert. He shot at it many times before it fell down dead. 'This was like no other bird I ever saw. It must have been the size of a horse,' he said.

thermal air currents   rising gusts of warm air

PTEROSAUR FACT FILE

One **species** of this reptile was:

- the largest flying creature of all time
- like a **vulture** that fed on dinosaur bodies
- bigger than a light aircraft.

The first **fossils** of this giant were found in 1972 in Texas.

FLYING MONSTER

In the days when **dinosaurs** lived, huge beasts also swept across the sky. One was like a giant hang-glider that drifted on air currents. It was called a pterosaur (*TERA-sore*) and its wingspan was over 12 metres. That is about the same as a small aeroplane! But like all flying **reptiles**, it became **extinct**. At least we think it did.

EVERYTHING IS BIG IN TEXAS!

In 1976 a police patrol car was driving through Brownsville, Texas, in the USA, early in the morning. It was just getting light. The two police officers suddenly looked up at a huge shadow in the sky. They could not believe their eyes. They could only shout into the radio.

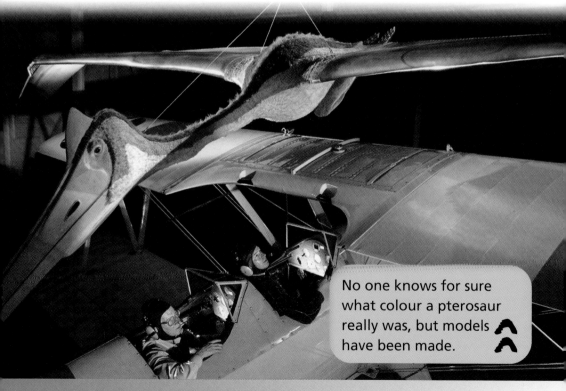

No one knows for sure what colour a pterosaur really was, but models have been made.

Aztec   ancient American-Indian civilization
species   type of living thing

OUT OF THIS WORLD

A short time later, a man in the same town heard thumping outside his home. When he looked out of the window, he saw a massive bird in his yard. 'It's like a bird, but it's not a bird,' he said. 'That animal is not from this world.'

MORE SIGHTINGS

More people said they had seen the 'flying monster'. Some teachers told of a large flying beast that dived at their cars as they drove to work. One of them rushed to the library and found a name for the animal: a pterosaur.

Things went quiet after that. The skies of Texas returned to normal. Until next time…

SURPRISE OF THE CIVIL WAR

US soldiers had a shock 130 years ago. A report tells how they shot down three pterodactyls. The pterodactyl is the pterosaur's cousin. It was all kept a big secret because no other details were known. Was it just a **hoax**? It is a real mystery.

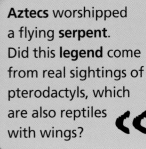

Aztecs worshipped a flying **serpent**. Did this **legend** come from real sightings of pterodactyls, which are also reptiles with wings?

THE HUGE BIRD

The Roc was a giant bird in **myths**, with feathers as big as palm leaves. It could carry an elephant in its claws and drop it from a great height. Some say it once lived on the island of Madagascar, in the Indian Ocean.

GIANT VULTURE

The largest bird that ever lived was a teratorn. It was as heavy as a man but it could still fly due to its huge wings. It would **soar** like a **condor** but it was far bigger. This giant **vulture** is supposed to have died out in the last ice age. But did it?

ALIVE IN ALASKA?

At the end of 2002, many people in Alaska reported seeing a strange bird. It was huge and looked nothing like an ordinary bird. They said it could not be one of the local sea birds. It was as big as a light aircraft. People said it looked like something out of the film *Jurassic Park*.

There are less than 100 Californian condors left in the wild. »

The Roc could carry off large animals like horses.

condor   very large vulture that lives in North and South America

IS IT A BIRD, IS IT A PLANE, IS IT A TERATORN?

The giant bird amazed people in the town of Togiak in Alaska. A pilot who lived there laughed when he heard the reports. He thought it must be a joke. But then he saw the bird just 300 metres away while he was flying his plane. 'He's huge, he's really, really big,' he said. 'You wouldn't want to have your children out.'

STILL A MYSTERY

The US Fish and Wildlife Service said there had been sightings over the past year of Steller's sea eagles in Alaska. These eagles are fish-eating birds that can have a wingspan of 2 to 3 metres. Even so, the mystery has not been solved.

The moa could not fly. »

THE EXTINCT GIANT MOA

The giant moa was one of the biggest birds ever known. It was over 3 metres tall and weighed 250 kilograms. In 1994, three hikers in the Craigieburn Mountains of New Zealand said they saw a live moa. It was reported round the world.

soar   fly high and glide in the sky
vulture   large bird that feeds on dead bodies

MONSTERS OF THE LAKE

FACT OR FICTION?

Some people say the Loch Ness monster is nonsense. It is all made up to boost the tourist trade in Scotland. They say it is just a giant eel, a seal or a big fish. They say the photos are a **hoax** or just show a log, a wave or an otter.

Thousands of lakes with deep murky water hide many secrets. Sometimes something stirs in the water… something huge.

THE LOCH NESS MONSTER

For over 1000 years, the mystery deep in Scotland's Loch Ness has brought monster hunters to find 'Nessie'. But it was only after a road was made round the **loch** about 70 years ago that so many people reported seeing the Loch Ness Monster.

FILM STAR?

It was then that a famous monster photo appeared. The world was amazed and wanted to know more about the creature with humps, a long tail and a head like a snake. The photo, shown on this page turned out to be a fake but still the search went on.

HUNDREDS OF REPORTS

Many people say they have seen a large head rise out of the loch. Some people say they have seen 'a huge beast with flippers' on the bank. There could be a whole family of mystery creatures **lurking** in the loch.

No otter has a neck this long!

loch   Scottish lake

THE HUNT GOES ON

One night a scientist in a small boat detected something with **sonar**. He said, 'rowing across that pitch-black water and knowing there was a very large animal just below my boat was frightening.'

Scientists have used mini-submarines, too. Now it is even possible to try to spy on Nessie using a web cam. How long will it be now before the Loch Ness Monster appears live on screen?

Fast fact

Go to www.lochness.co.uk/livecam and see if you can find Nessie on the live web cam.

Loch Ness is 39 km (24 miles) long and 2 km (1 mile) wide. In places it is deep enough to hide a 40-storey building.

In 1987 many boats scanned Loch Ness in the search for the monster. The sonar scans showed large shapes moving deep in the loch. They may have been huge fish. Or were they a family of monsters?

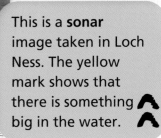

This is a **sonar** image taken in Loch Ness. The yellow mark shows that there is something big in the water.

A RUSSIAN COUSIN

A monster has been reported in Lake Kos in Russia. People claim it is 15 metres long with a head 2 metres long by 1 metre wide. Back in 1977, Moscow Radio reported that 'extinct' creatures may really have survived. 'Unknown creatures might still exist,' it said.

FAMILY

More than 250 of the world's lakes and rivers are reported to have some sort of mystery beast. Some of these are in other Scottish **lochs**. Nessie is not alone.

LEFT OVER AFTER MILLIONS OF YEARS?

People first learnt about **dinosaurs** in 1841. Before then, no one knew about 'water dinosaurs'. And yet for hundreds of years people described how Nessie looked. They told stories of a creature just like what we now know to be a **plesiosaur**. This was a large **reptile** with a neck up to 5 metres long. It had four large flippers, like wings to move it through water, and many teeth.

plesiosaur   large marine creature with paddle-like flippers and a long neck

DOUBTS

Could all of the lake monsters that have been reported really be plesiosaurs? Or could all the sightings over hundreds of years just be jokes? Is there more to the stories than that? There are still many questions and scientists still waiting for firm proof.

HOW TO GET RICH

A student took a video of what he said was a monster in Lake Van in Turkey. The creature was slimy and black and had horns on its head. But fuzzy film does not prove much. The world still waits for a clear film showing a real lake monster. But not a fake monster. People have tried to make millions from one of those.

A SWEDISH SECOND COUSIN

Lake Storsjön in Sweden is famous like Loch Ness. A large creature was first spotted there 350 years ago. Since 1987 there have been 400 reports of the 6-metre-long beast. It is grey-brown on top with a yellow belly.

Sometimes a playful seal can fool anyone!

OGOPOGO

There is supposed to be a monster called Ogopogo in Lake Okanagan in British Columbia, Canada. **Radar** has yet to find it once and for all. Perhaps the moving shadows are just a very large sturgeon fish. After all, sturgeon can grow up to 8 metres long.

AMERICAN LAKES

Canada and the USA are full of deep, dark lakes. Perhaps lakes are full of deep, dark monsters.

CHAMP

Lake Champlain borders New York and Vermont in the USA. It is over 160 kilometres (100 miles) long. As far back as 1609, people saw strange things in the water. In 1883, the Sheriff of Clinton County said he saw a fat snake 9 to 10 metres long in the lake. Then fishermen saw a large shape leave the water and crawl up the beach.

There is one photo of Champ, as the monster is now called. It looks like a **plesiosaur**. Other people have reported seeing it more recently.

This royal sturgeon was caught in the English Channel in 1947. It weighed over 180 kilograms – as much as a full-grown lion.

radar   using radio waves to find and track objects

TESSIE

Lake Tahoe in California is home to 'Tessie', a dark snake-like creature over 20 metres long. There is a film of 'something big' swimming in the lake but scientific searches have yet to find the monster. The Washoe Native Americans told stories in the 1800s of such a beast living in Lake Tahoe. Every year more people report a sighting of Tessie.

Manipogo may just be a huge, fierce fish like this.

No one can agree what Champ looks like. These are two possibilities.

MANIPOGO

There is another monster called Manipogo. It is said to live in Canada's Lake Manitoba. There have been reports of a huge snake-like creature in the lake since 1908. There is still no real proof – just a photo of a shape, but that could be anything.

35

A REAL MIX

In 1848, a bunyip was seen with a round head, a long neck and a body like an ox. Others said it was half horse and half crocodile, bigger than an elephant, with eyes like fire and tusks like a walrus.

THE BUNYIP

Bunyips are weird creatures. Australian **Aborigines** told of these beasts that are supposed to **lurk** in swamps, riverbeds and waterholes. The name bunyip means 'devil'. They come out at night with **blood-curdling** cries. They kill any animal or human that dares to come near. But the bunyip's favourite **prey** is meant to be women and children. Their tender flesh is just right and any shape or size will do. The bunyip is not choosy.

ALL SORTS

It seems that bunyips come in all shapes and sizes, with long tails or necks, wings, claws, horns, trunks, fur, **scales**, fins and feathers. But they all kill their prey by hugging it to death. What a way to go.

A large walrus can look like a bunyip.

blood-curdling   horrifying
culture   customs and traditions of the country

TASMANIA

In 1913, Oscar Davies saw a bunyip in Tasmania. He reported that the creature was about 5 metres long and 1.2 metres high, with a small head and thick neck. It had a shiny brown fur coat and four legs. The bunyip ran at great speed, leaving footprints that were 22 centimetres across. That does not sound like an average walrus.

LONG BLACK HAIR

Back in 1872 a man said he saw a bunyip in a **lagoon** at Wagga Wagga in Australia. He said it looked like 'a dog with really long black hair all over its body'. If ever a woman or child went missing, everyone used to fear the worst. Had a bunyip struck again? The good news is that there have not been many sightings lately.

JUST MYTH?

Whatever the bunyip really is, it has become a star of children's stories. It is now part of the **culture** in Australia. After looking at possible Bunyip bones and skulls, many Australians are sure the bunyip is pure **myth**.

Australian Aborigines traditionally hunted in lagoons and waterholes. Did they spot bunyips in the water? ❯❯

lagoon   saltwater lake by the sea
prey   victim to be killed and eaten

MONSTERS OF THE SEAS

MONSTER OF THE WAVES

A bishop from Norway was on his way to Greenland in 1734. A massive sea serpent raised its head from the sea – as high as the ship's mast. When it fell back into the waves, the bishop said its tail was longer than the ship itself.

There were no cameras in the 1700s so people made carvings of the monsters they claimed to have seen.

Sailors through the ages have told scary tales about sea **serpents**. Maybe on long voyages they had nothing better to do than make up **far-fetched** stories. Unless, of course, the stories were true.

HMS *DAEDALUS*

In 1848, seven sailors aboard the ship *Daedalus* saw a strange creature in the ocean as the ship sailed near Cape Town in South Africa. The captain said it was a 14-metre long sea serpent. It swam beside the ship for about 20 minutes. The monster's head was a metre out of the water and its jaws were big enough to eat a man in one gulp. Everyone on board the ship was terrified.

The frilled shark is one of the strangest looking sea creatures. Its long thin body and large gaping mouth make it particularly serpent-like.

THE SEA SERPENT OF GLOUCESTER

For over 300 years, hundreds of people have told stories about the sea serpent of Gloucester port in the USA. In 1817, **shipmaster** Allen wrote about the sea serpent:

'His head was like a rattlesnake's, but as large as the head of a horse. He slowly moved on the surface of the water in circles.'

SHOT

Another sailor shot at the serpent and said, *'I took good aim at his head. I must have hit him. He turned towards me after I had fired, and I thought he was coming at us. But he sank down and went directly under our boat.'*

LOOK-ALIKE

The oarfish is an eel-like animal that can be over 8 metres long – maybe even double this size. It is silver with bright red spikes running down its back. Two men killed a giant one near Bermuda in 1860. They thought it was a sea serpent.

Has an oarfish like this been mistaken for a monster?

TYPES OF SEA MONSTERS REPORTED

1 Merhorse: large eyes, smooth skin and a mane

2 Multi-humped: whale-like with several humps

3 Long-necked: small head and four flippers

4 Super eel: giant eel-like fish, no limbs

5 Yellow belly: tadpole-shaped, yellow with a black stripe

ATLANTIC MONSTER

You may see a sea monster called Chessie where the Chester River meets the sea near Baltimore in the USA. Now and again a ripple moves across calm water. A black creature 10 metres long pops its head up. A **witness** once said, 'The eye looked like a serpent's. It didn't look like a fish.'

Sometimes groups of people see Chessie. In 1980, 25 people in four boats saw Chessie at the same time. In 1982 Robert Frew filmed a long, dark creature swimming in Chesapeake Bay. It was about 10 metres long with a humped back. Then it dived under some swimmers. They soon swam to shore.

This map shows where sea monsters have been spotted in the USA.

Key to map
- ᕫᕫᕫ Caddy
- ᕫᕫᕫ Chessie
- ᕫᕫᕫ Port Gloucester sea serpent

Seattle

Chicago

Boston

New York

Washington D.C.

USA

Los Angeles

Atlantic Ocean

Pacific Ocean

Gulf of Mexico

witness   someone who is there when something happens

PACIFIC MONSTER

Caddy is a sea monster that is supposed to live off the north-west coast of North America. It has been popping up for over 1000 years. So people say. They also say that:

- it is between 5 and 15 metres long
- its body is snake-like, with a neck of 4 metres
- its head is said to be like that of a sheep, horse, giraffe or camel
- it has a pair of front flippers
- its tail is spiky
- it can swim very fast.

People still say they see it around Vancouver Island in Canada. But what is it? Caddy remains a mystery.

QUESTIONS

What is Caddy? No one really knows. It could be a sea **dinosaur** from long ago. Maybe it is a type of whale we do not know about. The coast of North America is **remote** and borders one of the deepest undersea trenches in the world. Who knows what might hide there?

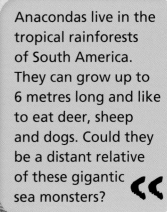

Anacondas live in the tropical rainforests of South America. They can grow up to 6 metres long and like to eat deer, sheep and dogs. Could they be a distant relative of these gigantic sea monsters? **‹‹**

GIANT SQUID

Giant squid live deep in the ocean. These huge creatures are hardly ever seen, so we still know very little about them. Sometimes a dead giant squid is washed up on to a beach.

A giant squid can be as big as two buses. Its eyes are half a metre across – the largest eyes in the world.

In 2003 a giant squid was caught in the Antarctic. It was the first time Dr O'Shea had seen its five pairs of long arms with suckers and hooks. 'It has to be one of the most frightening **predators** out there,' he said.

They can kill whales, so a human would just be a snack.

Giant squid sometimes wash up onto beaches.

THE SS *TRESCO*

In 1903 the *SS Tresco* was sailing off the North Carolina coast. A sailor wrote:

'I saw something with a 30-metre body. The head was the size of a man. Our ship was in danger of tipping over if it tried to clamber aboard.'

predator   animal that hunts and eats other creatures

GIANT OCTOPUS

A cousin of the squid is the octopus but this monster has eight arms. It lives on the seabed, up to several kilometres deep. Octopuses come in a range of sizes but the question is, 'How big can they get?'

Some sailors believe a giant octopus exists. It could weigh 10 tonnes and measure over 30 metres across. That is a giant! An octopus half this size was found dead in 1896 on a Florida beach. Even this was a monster as big as a house.

The giant octopus may be the creature behind the kraken, which appears in Norwegian **myths**. Stories tell how the dreaded kraken could sink a ship and eat all the crew.

MYSTERY MONSTER

In 1964, Robert Serrec was on holiday in Australia. In shallow sea off Queensland, he saw a tadpole-like creature about 25 metres long. It seemed to have a wound on its back. He took pictures of the creature before it swam off. It was not seen again.

This is one of Robert Serrec's photos of a giant tadpole-like creature. ❮❮

The harmless basking shark is often mistaken for a sea monster. It is one of the largest fish in the sea – it can be over 12 metres long. ❮❮

MYSTERIES OF THE FOREST

DEEP AND MYSTERIOUS

The Congo is a **vast** area. The thick forests have not changed for thousands of years. They could still hide animals we have never seen. In 1959, a pilot looked down on a huge snake over 15 metres long. Its massive head looked as if it was from another world.

There are secrets hiding deep in the swamps, jungles and long underground caves of Africa. There is a large country called The Democratic Republic of Congo, where people have seen signs of a monster for over 200 years. Few people go deep into the dark **water-logged** forests. They call the monster *Mokele-mbembe*. It means 'the one who stops the river'.

Local people believe the monster is **sacred**. They say a tribe once killed a *Mokele-mbembe*. Many ate its meat and died so perhaps the beast has a **curse**. Now everyone keeps well away from the monster's thick swamp.

What monsters lurk in the swamps of the Congo? **>>**

WEIRD WORDS   **bulky**   of stocky build – large and awkward
pillar   solid column that helps support a building

BAD TEMPER

The mystery beast is bigger than an elephant, but with a long neck and short legs. It has smooth, brown skin and spends a lot of time in water. Although it does not eat meat, it will attack humans or hippos. The monster seems to be very moody and does not like to be disturbed. It is said that *Mokele-mbembe* will overturn boats and kill people by biting and hitting them with its tail. Hippos keep well away from these monsters.

LIVING DINOSAUR?

Big footprints with three claws have been found around the swamps. Some scientists think there may be a type of **dinosaur** here called a sauropod. But so far there is no real proof.

SAUROPOD DINOSAURS

These were plant-eating **reptiles**. They had small heads and little brains. Their bodies were **bulky**, with four **pillar**-like legs. They had long necks and tails. Dinosaurs were the largest animals on the Earth millions of years ago. Some sauropods may have been 35 metres long and weighed 100 tonnes!

Lake Tele and Likoula Swamp may hide a creature only seen by a few people.

sacred very special or holy
water-logged flooded with water

FAMILY

The tree sloth lives in the Amazon rainforest. It hangs from trees and moves very slowly from branch to branch. Although it is the nearest living relative of the giant ground sloth, it is tiny when compared with its huge **extinct** cousin.

THE AMAZON MONSTER

Even in the 21st century, we still do not know all the creatures that live on our planet. Many kilometres of thick jungle still keep big beasts hidden. The Amazon rainforest is among the largest in the world and there may be monsters hiding deep inside.

One such beast has a strange name as well as a strange smell. It is the Mapinguari, a giant ground sloth. Tree sloths are hairy ape-like creatures that move very slowly in trees. But giant ground sloths were very different. They once roamed over all America, until for some reason they died out a few thousand years ago. But maybe not *all* of them died.

The tree sloth is only about 70 cm tall. It spends most of its life upside-down in trees.

A BAD SMELL

This rare animal is said to have stood several metres tall. It had long red-brown hair. Over 50 people say they have seen a Mapinguari in the last 30 years. One **witness** was Mário de Souza, who came across a giant sloth along a river in Brazil in 1975. He said, 'The horrible smell hit me and made me dizzy. I was not right for two months.'

This Cambodian stamp shows the Mapinguari.

Some Brazilian **foresters** swear they have seen Mapinguari kill men by twisting off their heads and cracking open their skulls. This may seem **far-fetched**, but why would foresters lie? They are people who normally stay calm and keep their heads.

EXTINCT?

Giant ground sloths lived a few thousand years ago in the Americas. One fossil is 6 metres high, like an elephant that could stand on two legs. It was a megatherium. Could the mystery beast in the Amazon be a megatherium still alive today?

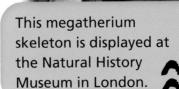

This megatherium skeleton is displayed at the Natural History Museum in London.

MONSTER OF SOUTH AMERICA

In 1999, Brazil's *Corriero* newspaper reported eight goats and three sheep dying of wounds to the neck. Other Brazilian **witnesses** claimed to have seen an animal that can fly or leap with strong, monkey-like legs. It is said to attack animals and humans.

CHUPACABRA

Imagine a vampire mixed with a Bigfoot. This monster could be the *chupacabra* from the South American rainforest. It seems to visit the USA, too.

A REPORT FROM 2002

A boy told how he met a chupacabra in Salt Lake City in the USA. 'We got to my friend's farm and turned on the porch lights. There was growling behind us and I saw a monkey-like creature with no tail and glowing eyes. It ran off into the woods. My friend followed but it chased him out again. Later my friend found his two goats dead. They were drained of blood, with bite marks in their necks. His dog went missing and was never found.'

Goats seem to be the Chupacabra's favourite food.

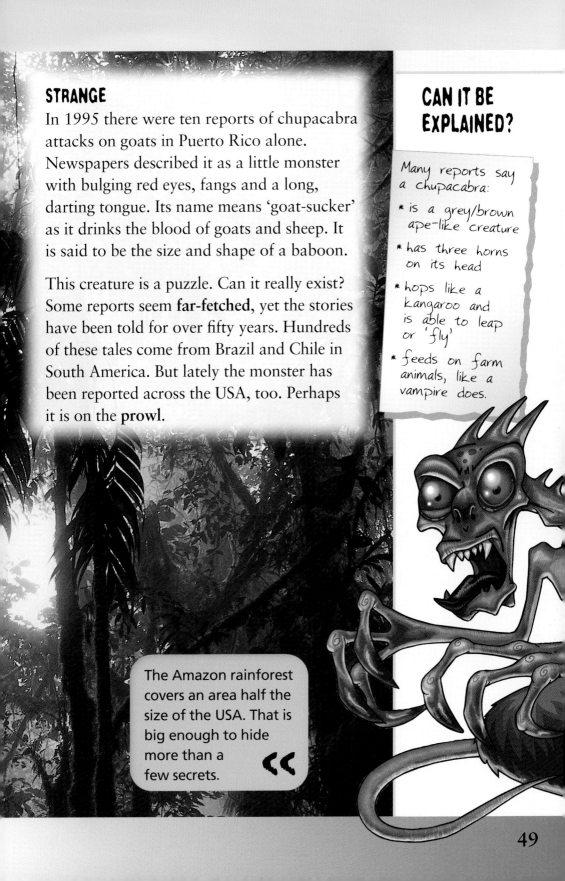

STRANGE

In 1995 there were ten reports of chupacabra attacks on goats in Puerto Rico alone. Newspapers described it as a little monster with bulging red eyes, fangs and a long, darting tongue. Its name means 'goat-sucker' as it drinks the blood of goats and sheep. It is said to be the size and shape of a baboon.

This creature is a puzzle. Can it really exist? Some reports seem **far-fetched**, yet the stories have been told for over fifty years. Hundreds of these tales come from Brazil and Chile in South America. But lately the monster has been reported across the USA, too. Perhaps it is on the **prowl**.

CAN IT BE EXPLAINED?

Many reports say a chupacabra:

* is a grey/brown ape-like creature

* has three horns on its head

* hops like a kangaroo and is able to leap or 'fly'

* feeds on farm animals, like a vampire does.

The Amazon rainforest covers an area half the size of the USA. That is big enough to hide more than a few secrets. "

49

LAND OF THE GIANTS

THE FIRST OF ITS KIND

The Lost World was the first story about dinosaurs. It was about a man searching the jungle for a hidden **plateau**. He had heard that the plateau was locked in the past. It was a lost world with monsters from another age. What he found in this world has sparked our imaginations ever since.

Monsters once ruled the Earth. Now we think humans do. But maybe there really are a few monsters still **lurking** out there. After all, people often say they see them. Is it just their minds playing tricks? Is it all a bit of fun? Or do some people want to believe in monsters so much that they make themselves see them? Maybe someone will soon show real proof that one of these mysterious creatures exists.

We are still finding out about huge **dinosaurs** that lived millions of years ago. The first story about them was written in 1912 by Arthur Conan Doyle. It was called *The Lost World*.

A scene from *The Lost World* where the explorers' dinner is stolen by a pterodactyl. **>>**

WEIRD WORDS   clone   breed an exact copy of a creature using its DNA

SCIENCE FACT OR FICTION?

Ever since *The Lost World* came out, books and films have made us worry. What if dinosaurs are still alive? What if they come back?

Maybe it could happen. After all, scientists keep finding bodies of **extinct** creatures in ice or in tar pits. They are taken to laboratories and their cells are studied. One day scientists hope to make new life from the **DNA** they find in these cells. They are already trying to **clone** a baby mammoth. Perhaps it is just a matter of time before extinct monsters walk again.

Maybe the mysterious monsters of the past are already on their way back…

The dinosaurs in today's films look like the real thing.

JURASSIC PARK AND ANOTHER LOST WORLD

In 1990, Michael Crichton wrote *Jurassic Park*. It is about theme park dinosaurs that begin to attack humans. This book made dinosaur stories popular again.

His next book had a familiar title – the same as 83 years before. It was *The Lost World*. Once more, monsters were fighting back!

plateau   piece of land that is raised up higher than the land around it

FIND OUT MORE

MONSTER WEBSITES

WALKING WITH DINOSAURS

Step-by-step guide to dinosaur myths and legends.
bbc.co.uk/dinosaurs

YETI HUNTING

Photographs and games about the yeti.
legendofyeti.com

DINORAMA

Excellent guide to dinosaurs with the latest dinosaur news.
nationalgeographic. com/dinorama

BOOKS

Can Science Solve? The Mystery of the Abominable Snowman, Chris Oxlade and Anita Ganeri (Heinemann Library, 1999)

Can Science Solve? The Mystery of the Loch Ness Monster, Chris Oxlade and Anita Ganeri (Heinemann Library, 1999)

WORLD WIDE WEB

If you want to find out more about **monsters**, you can search the Internet using keywords like these:

- monster + Frankenstein
- 'Komodo Dragon'
- megalania + skull
- vampires + [name of a country]
- 'Loch Ness Monster'

You can also find your own keywords by using headings or words from this book. Use the search tips opposite to help you find the most useful websites.

SEARCH TIPS

There are billions of pages on the Internet so it can be difficult to find exactly what you are looking for. If you just type in 'monster' on a search engine like Google, you will get a list of 8 million web pages. These search skills will help you find useful websites more quickly:

- Know exactly what you want to find out
- Use simple keywords, not whole sentences
- Use two to six keywords in a search
- Be precise – only use names of people, places or things
- If you want to find words that go together, put quote marks around them
- Use the + sign to add certain words, for example typing monster + games into the search box will help you find web pages with games related to monsters.

SEARCH ENGINE

A search engine looks through the entire web and lists all the sites that match the words in the search box. The best matches are at the top of the list, on the first page. Try **bbc.co.uk/search**

SEARCH DIRECTORY

A search directory is like a library of websites. You can search by keyword or subject and browse through the different sites like you would look through books on a shelf. A good example is **yahooligans.com**

GLOSSARY

abominable terrible, disgusting

Aborigine native culture of Australia

ambush surprise attack

ancient from a past age long ago

Australian bush Australia's wild country, with desert, scrub land and swamps

Aztec ancient American-Indian civilization

bleak bare, cold and windy

blood-curdling horrifying

boar large wild pig

bulky of stocky build – large and awkward

business trade for making money

clone breed an exact copy of a creature using its DNA

condor very large vulture that lives in North and South America

culture customs and traditions of a country

curse strange power that brings harm to some people

Dark Ages over 1000 years ago, when people knew little about the world or science

dinosaur big 'terrible lizard' from prehistoric times

DNA individual code locked in the genes that shows the make-up of a creature

evidence information that can help prove if something is true or false

extinct died out, never to return

fantasy from the world of dreams and imagination

far-fetched over the top and rather hard to believe

fiction made-up story from the imagination

folklore old beliefs, myths and stories

forester someone who plants and manages forests

fossils ancient remains of animal bones and teeth

glinted sparkled with light

habitat natural home or environment

hoax untrue story made up for a joke

hostile unfriendly or against you

lagoon saltwater lake by the sea

legend story from long ago that may be partly true

loch Scottish lake

lurking waiting around, ready to strike

maiden young unmarried woman

myth made-up tale, told over many years

pillar solid column that helps support a building

plateau piece of land that is raised up higher than the land around it

plesiosaur large marine creature with paddle-like flippers and a long neck

predator animal that hunts and eats other creatures

prey hunt down to kill; victim to be killed and eaten

prowl creep about hunting for prey

rabies disease caught from the bite of an infected animal

radar using radio waves to find and track objects

reliable sensible and trustworthy

remote far away from people

reptiles cold-blooded creatures that lay eggs, like snakes and lizards

sacred very special or holy

saliva mouth juices, spit

scales small bony plates that protect the skin – found on fish and reptiles

serpent large snake

shipmaster guard in charge of the harbour

slay kill

soar fly high and glide in the sky

sonar using sound waves to detect objects under water

species type of living thing

stake stick or post sharpened at one end

stench foul smell

stirred start to move after being asleep or still for some time

survived stayed alive despite the dangers

talons claws of a bird of prey

thermal air currents rising gusts of warm air

triumph success and victory

vast very large area

vile really revolting

vulture large bird that feeds on dead bodies

water-logged flooded with water

witness someone who is there when something happens

yak long-haired mountain ox

INDEX